# Claytown

## JAMES GOODMAN

**SALT**

LONDON

PUBLISHED BY SALT PUBLISHING
Acre House, 11–15 William Road, London NW1 3ER, United Kingdom

© James Goodman, 2011

The right of James Goodman to be identified as the
author of this work has been asserted by him in accordance
with Section 77 of the Copyright, Designs and Patents Act 1988.

Salt Publishing 2011

Printed and bound in the United Kingdom by CPI Anthony Rowe

Typeset in Swift 9.5 / 13

ISBN 978 1 84471 259 5 paperback

Salt Publishing Ltd gratefully acknowledges
the financial assistance of Arts Council England

1 3 5 7 9 8 6 4 2

# Claytown

JAMES GOODMAN grew up in St Austell, Cornwall, near the Clay Country landscapes described in *Claytown*. He works for a sustainable development charity and lives in Hertfordshire with his wife and son. This is his first collection.

# Contents

# Claytown

# Helman Tor

When the old moon smoked itself red,
when it curdled at its leading edge
then burst apart, when it spumed
over Gemini and a swathe of Taurus
and the powder cake cascade
poured down, this sheepshit tor,
this snag in the weather's tumble
rose up to meet it.

The clitter's quartz gleamed,
caught the magpies' ragged eyes.
And below the hill,
beyond the tin-stream eddies,
between the reeling, stunted oaks,
hidden in the grass beside the oily reed-marsh,
a giant puffball, braced with spores, looked up,
the muddy eyeball of another moon.

# The catch

One of them spotted a broken gannet
on the upslip of a wave. They sculled over
and saw it was a man, frozen in a storm

of wax, with eagle feathers struck about him
and his arms and legs angled in fright
so he looked like an archaeopteryx,

flawed and ancient. They pulled alongside
and cracked open the wax to let him breathe
and the weight of air rushed into his lungs.

In the boat, they listened to his story.
And they told how last May they'd picked up
a roe buck while out fishing mackerel

full two miles offshore, rolled him onboard
just the same as today, and he'd sprung off
from the beach as if nothing had happened.

## We have yet to harness the full potential of clouds

he said, and there they were, brazen, tripping over the brow, utterly free in their stream, *our Government will seize them and privatise them and they'll be tradeable property. People will use them for storage, transit, real-estate, ad space, disposal, barter, leverage, silage, tillage, bondage, homage, garage, we'll illuminate our rooms with them, build among them gleaming sails to live beneath, use them in the manufacture of cams, cabrioles, capacitors, we'll hang walkways between them, hitch and follow them in their twirl over sea and land, they'll be our music, our cirrus strings, long stratus bows, we'll stick needles in them, mine them for their vital succulence, use them to perform staggering calculations,* and there they were, brazen, tripping over the brow of the hill, scatty and light and free and utterly unsuspecting.

# Deer

All through the trip I'd been looking for them
out across the scarp and blow,
glancing first to far corners of fields,
along the quick recourse of woodland edges,
or in each glimpse of sunken country lane
expecting their still otherness to thrill me.
I even conjured them myself—a branch
thickened into something rapt and tense;
ghosts scattered down the lines of hedges
as we scudded past the scour of hills and new estates.
But nothing, until the outskirts of the town,
and a torn-up verge by Furniture Village,
where they stood in elegant assembly,
a well-made table and two empty chairs.

# St Genies

Collared doves, warm mizzle, chimes from the clock-
tower at the end of the lane—

the pear tree sickening with summer, cutting loose
its basketful of skulls—

the tied-up goat fixed in a sphere of devastation
whose radius is a tether's length.

# Cherry blossom

The cherry blossom stutters
all through winter,

shapes the vowel-sounds of spring
far too early,

snags on December's interruption
of November.

The new year starts with outright
mispronunciation.

The blossom parties are a joke;
there's no fruit come autumn.

# Snowflake

They bob around in the freezing cloud-forge
miles up in the night, meeting and joining hands,
until their weight is snagged and they fall.

How comforting to drift to ground like that,
in such company, holding each other's
stellar arms, like sky-divers over Texas

who giddy and spin through the fickle air
and laugh into each other's crystal eyes.
And how comforting to land among friends

and at the point of impact, wait a while,
not go quite yet, look about and see
who joined the long hug of the gentle hedge,

who gave the granite scratching-post its quiff,
who settled on the bull's steaming flank
as it stood alone in the middle of the field.

# Easter Sunday in the Clay

Up to the silence of bank-holiday clayworks, silence of south-season gorse downs, early butterflies. Herring gulls blown inland on high air, their cries picking out silence and hectares. Machine track rolling the hunch of moor like a spine, up to the bewildered line of sky-tips, far off, legend-strides. Through the gap in the blown hedge. Earth pending, white earth tottering over Great Longstone, Littlejohns, Gunheath, Dorothy, grit-bitten earth, salt-shocked earth. Gleaming elements of earth, growling tread-marks bitten in the white grit. Silence of still diggers on the ridge, menhirs' cold shift of years. Silence, waiting for beeps to reverse off the cliff again, wind to carry back the engine whirrs, the clay-rock canyon to snag the gears' echo; the dyspeptic gorge to flow, mica to glint in the slurry stream, words refill the diggers' cabins. White silt down in the estuary, new washing land.

# Claytown

Remember the evening we measured ourselves against each other, in the long-shadow field that shears off Tregorrick, prone beneath every dusk that's thrown across the disaster sky of Carclaze and Scredda, their map of pits and tips. We lay back and watched our town decline, gardens slump into unrecorded mines, shops fall in on piles of mail, darkness rise to meet what was there, as the end of the sun slipped through the cliffs of sky and the cough of malt from the brewery keened on the air. When the run of booze dried, we skeltered down the lane on bikes, night-blind and brakeless, shouting to hear the hedges near and the crook at the end, down to the white lake where the clay waste's settled to dry. *It's mica dam or mikey dam, is it mica or mikey, the white mud lake? If it's a boy, Mikey, Mica if it's a girl.*

# In the emptiest square on the map

You'll find no wandering orange line
or mark for saltings, heath or boundary stone.
Though you might have expected a sky webbed
by telegraph poles, a car turned into the ground,

trails of wire, white flags, a wash of starlings,
they won't be there. The beetle moving north
by north by north has gone. Even the grass
has blown from its circumference of wind.

It's three hours' train ride, a cab for five miles more,
five hundred paces further. You'll travel alone.
All that's there is you, your body's dark stare
and the years escaping with a whooshing sound.

# The White Hill

*Sterile as the moon—windrush of larksong—the pit at work—a shadow of*
*dust—the water-cannon jet—clay-slurry froth—great wash of noise—water-*
*shattered—the pitworks rotating—lode of clay—clench of rock—excavator*
*trudge—rag-edged tracks—even at night—the assault of light—thrown*
*into the sky—gusting quiet—then eruption of noise—scraped out land—the*
*land's true line—hard to discern—between pit and sky-tip—sign for the*
*next blast—date and stope—danger-zone/time—this pit went post-*
*industrial in July—*

≈

In the beginning was the pluton
lobing from the molten mass, forcing up
the interlocking shales, a slow flare
rising from the planet's mantle.

The magma cooled and clenched as granite—
vuggy, trail-swarmed with quartz,
feldspar-heavy, scattered with mica.
Then water entered its stress-joints and faults,

rode the fissures into its heart, travelled
the tourmaline veins, invading the tight mass.
The granite softened in its killas nest
and the feldspar, sated with brine, changed,

loosened off the hard mineral bones, withered
and steamed and rotted, and the rot spread,
a bloom that would shine white when the crust
of soil broke, exposing china clay.

≈

*The clay road a white flag—hillslabs effaced—marquetry of sands—the*
*land tips away—into bloodless scarp—dunes scurry grit—hammer-marks*

*in the pit—drilled, pocked granite—track-chiselled scope—lagoon in the*
*sump—the claywater blue—toothpaste blue—a frequency effect—of*
*nanoscale particles—residue suspended in this quarry-bight—a settling*
*time of decades—*

~

The spent village of Greensplat
on a slip of hard-edged land
between the pits of Great Longstone
and Wheal Martyn China Clay Works.

On the high hill by Carrancarrow
half a dozen squat homes
hedged up against the road
slack-leashed with telegraph lines,

a grey-slate Methodist chapel,
clay-dust telephone box,
steel-lattice transmission mast,
wide scandal of turned earth.

A shambling path through
a dock-and-daisy field
with goats and chicken-wire
breaks the hedge and meets the pit-void.

~

*Clay-mud stagnants—one colour then the next—finger-march of*
*lichens—soft remittances of moss—point-by-point inheritance of reeds—at*
*the pit-mere's edge—sterile quartz-sand then—a rainbow of greens—skim*
*of ages—time like water—foxglove marshal—the pit a bowl—growing*
*strains—two feral goats graze the colonised stent—cuckoo sounding the*

*silence of the pit—a band of goldfinches bounces past—uniforms gaudy*
*against the greys and whites—*

~

This new hill's undesired
twelve tiers growing out of grey
and into green, warren-shot,

as steep as a roof.
On a dry day we climbed
the sand-washed

gulley, pulled our way
up with hazel-stalks
and fists of yellow grass

past shit-scattered burrows
to the summit: a kestrel perch
on a sky-dagger,

vole-magnifying views.
The hare's loop
of Dartmoor, forty miles east,

the long slip of Carnmenellis
twenty miles to the west,
their slow granite hunches,

and the ellipsis of moon-dishes at Goonhilly—
Watch Hill's new perspective
from the certainty of waste,

of rebellious farms

lines of woods, trees,
the grey-green scribble of fields.

～

This *overburden*,
call it tumult of flesh,
the soil's thin story of
tribulations, gridlines,

the wrack of heather
the clutch of gorse
and closer by, the road's
shoreline of grit and shoes.

Below the freight of soil
below the ageing humus
below the archaeology
the coins and pot-shards

below the scum to be lifted
from the rotten rock:
the whitened granite,
kaolin's buried gleam.

～

*Ulex galli—ulex europeaus—lupinus arboreus—rumex acetosa—digitalis
purpurea—lamium purpureum—calluna vulgaris—osmunda regalis—*

～

This is where we came
to watch the eclipse
in '99,

the shadow-drama
of the decade:

the makeshift carpark
of the field
beneath the white hill,

cars spun into mud, doors
left open

crowds of witnesses
in the lowering mizzle

strato-cumulus
seamless with the sky's edge.

The darkness marched eastward,
the moon — track-rutted — pit-gaped —
moving its shadow

quickly up the far-away coast
towards us

(the line between light and dark
hard to discern)

the wash of gloom
and with it, a sparkling wake,

mica-scatter of
flashbulbs, tiny points

of misdirected light
illuminating shade

and then the inevitable lightening.

# The cause of thunder

The Earth rolls in its socket

and the field, a green iris

The air is moody, its clouds

I hear the sound of air being pulled

They meet the earth and start to mix

tell soon enough my direction

a line of light opens in the dark pupil

recoils and focusses.

flickering on the edge of sight—

through air, as the clouds propagate.

and I can read the sky's exegesis,

wind-lashed as the wiry maples.

## As for the components of the face

**glabella—**
midpoint, thumbprint, pivot,
cross-mark of the line from crown
to jaw and ear to ear
unmoving eye
in the storm of your expression

**nasalabial sulcus—**
telling furrow, faultline
where the lip subducts
beneath the cheek
that time will curve and deepen
in microcosmic quakes and shifts

**philtrum—**
ski-jump, touching crest,
exponent of the rise from doubtful lip
to the singularity of nose
launch-pad
for your first experiment with flight

# Sap rising

There were cats screwing all over the place,
it was one of those summers.
Hers had disappeared, poor Xerxes
the ancient waddler, the fat-balled tom

who turned up at a dozen houses to be fed
and had as many names. Hence
the aunt-recommended crystal-dowser,
crunched over the map of London

on the recovered-wood kitchen table,
swinging his claw of cheesy quartz.
He wasn't sure, but a certain street
in Bounds Green provoked a reaction.

They ended up in an allotment hot
with lemon mint and so dense with ley-lines
their arteries were twitching with the force.
She defied first-kiss convention

by sucking his lower lip very hard,
as if there was something in there
she needed desperately for herself—which
she knew at the time to be quite wrong.

# Spring, when it came

With time-lapse indecency, the backed-up sap in the unsprung coils of tuber and bulb boiled through stems and fizzed out. Leaves, forced through the sleeves of twigs, gestured for their falcons to hunt down light, which blazed from the birds' plumes as they returned. Bracken punched its fists through winter's tarmac. New roots screwed the earth down to its shelf of rock while daffodils cracked into flower, splitting air. Bluebell grass sweated in its welter of glade. Pushed for time, flowers pressed on till dawn, working the dark and the giddy moths. The season changed like a shock of wood-pigeon clearing the trees. A line of wreckage moved up the map in black and white, breaking the frost of November and burying winter. The pomp of its announcement! Leaves were sheaves of fire, trees furled their lozenges of semtex; though winter has strength in depth, deliberating its constitution of darkness, its sunk inches of soil.

# Limoncello

What are you doing there,
unopened bottle of sunlight,
shining out from the most awkward cupboard
where the tenants before

the tenants before left you?
Forgotten flame in boozy shadow,
there beside the popcorn-maker
owlet-furred with dust and grease

burning with the waxy yellow light
of two short weeks away
those people you won't meet again
thought they wanted to prolong.

Abandoned and unopened, not opened,
never opened, never once even opened.
Come with me and we'll spend the night,
relive someone else's well-earned break.

*Best drunk alone or with ice.*

# Avian

Black metal
taking sparks off the sky's flint.

Break the sky open: there's night,
with its unseen shine.

(swift)

∽

Starlight in the oak's
bare reaches —

have you ever seen
stars chattering like that?

(long-tailed tit)

∽

Inform the wind-eddy of trash
over the distant woods
that the apocalypse has started.

(rook)

∽

Some huge beauty
lifts from the field.

Three flaps, then turns
its atlas pages to the sun.

(buzzard)

～

Just a sense of absence
on the pillar of bridge

cleanly torn air
an eye's pixel misfiring.

(kingfisher)

～

Cloistered on this so-cold day
and still as flares, lilac and rose,
the frosted wavelets of the field.

(woodpigeon)

～

What's left is turned to wavelength
of gristle, sputum, spasm, glister, mucus,
tendon, glimmer,        sky and shimmer.

(starling)

∾

except here, hidden deep
in the pied winter

one feathered patch
opening its red flesh

(greater spotted
woodpecker)

# The snow estate

The snow estate is the longest kiss of forgiveness,
tracing every creak and ledge of its enemy's profile.

It is something to envy, an embrace that touches all points,
each snagged flake its own sparkle of compassion.

Though see how forgiveness melts eventually,
beginning with the track-lines of cars on gritted roads,

receding to reveal again the jags and turrets
of the true landscape, harsh, pedantic, unrelenting.

OS

Bracken, heath, rough grassland, sand and shingle, *important building*, church with spire. Windmill, with or without sails. *Ferry* P—passenger only. Narrow road with passing places, danger area, visible earthwork, milepost, cutting, clubhouse. The blush of orchards, complexion of sands, poignant scree, swamp-contusions. B-road crossed with c-road crossed with d-road, and polygons of space. Flatlands of dither where bridleways surge, public paths spin, and borders, boundaries and frontiers arrange *civil parishes*. Here is the glamour of woods sunk in clutches, where contours muscle-bunch streams, tighten round valleys, but let the water slip, the valley burst with woodland shapes, coniferous, deciduous and mixed. Mud shows where a break-out over fields followed a trudge-line through mire, when rain rode a gale along the broken coast, the lost car leaking its light into a bluster. Fold-lines, channelling all of these lives, dirtied with what they describe.

# Blackbird

You are the engine of the bush
You are the ripple of the moon
You are the spinney's lonely bell
You are the shooting of the eye

You are an easel made of bark
You are the orbit of the morning
You are the welter of the evening
You are the evening of the sky

You are a footmark in the snow
You are the path between the woods
You are the quickness in the spinney
You are the clearing from the west

You are the falling of the leaf
You are the *hira-hira* sound
You are a scribble in still air
You are the compass of the threat

You are a shudder in the bush
You are the softening of the branch
You are the grammar of the copse
You are the pebbling of fright

You are a breath inside a breath
You are the shoreline of the rain
You are the target of the air
You are the harness of the night

You are the whistle-maker's thought
You are the tick-tock song of want
You are the conversation's start
You are the cause of the dissent

# The buzz

The silence ends abruptly with a blur
through the open kitchen door,
its hundred heartbeats a second
ranging the room like a worry.

I divert its course with a newspaper flap
and it alights on *What is History?* by E.H. Carr,
'his acclaimed reflections on the theory
of history and the role of the historian'—

a book that I've not opened
for a decade. The fly rests there,
its foremost legs twitching,
rubbing perfumes on its head.

I move like moss in the shadow
of a standing stone. I am stone,
and I move with the edging certainty
of the continental plates.

# Beside the Draa

Mesdames and messieurs
hear how our donkey's hollow bleat
resounds through the palmery

and how the two sad syllables
of another seem to answer
from far away.

Donkeys send out echoes of loss
throughout the oasis
and who can blame them?

I have heard how once they
frolicked on fragrant plains,
chattering in ancient light.

# The wishing well

one a shadow of rain
one a shelf of keys
one a spray of little dawns
one a comb of ribs
one a curdled dagger
one a ripple's breaking edge

the ferns and their reflections
in the well-pool
nod in the rain
as the two waters meet

one a drench of holy water
one a coomb of rain
one a handshake of arrows
one a fossil blade
one a shadow of daggers
one a quiver of slate

# Contours

Tethered to gravity's billow and waft
they track, turn, race across the map,
pulse, swerve and flock, edge the plateaux,
force the bulging hills upwards

with their tightening grip. They scope
the land as if they were creating it
move together but rarely touch.
Each is numbered, each joins only itself.

They hide in woodlands and towns,
seem to slow their practised glide
and stall in the blockage of symbols,
tarry in the streets and multi-storey carparks.

Then they're out and on their way to the coast,
chasing down the valley sides
till they stumble at the cliff-edge cordon,
crowding the extent of their oblivion.

# Pilchard-fishing

The shadow arrives, untethered from its storm-cloud

drawing strikes of gannets from the sky, and a rain of eyes.

The shoal turns, and from the cliff the water phase-shifts,

takes the sky's black and darkness from the land

and rolls them together beneath the waves

(the birds are awkward fish, their scissor-beaks cutting at foil).

Water slick with oil, except the shallows where it fizzes pilchard-red,

so the *huers* as they stride the bay's spores and bracken

shout out *hevva*, meaning shoal, calling the launch of boats—

seine boats, anchor boats, follower boats, tourist boats—

and semaphore their strategy with gorse-brush and smocks

to haul the summer catch close in to shore

where they find the shadow disaggregates, barrels from the seines with ease

and baulks in cobbled fish-palaces, layering with salt,,

the overflow in oil lamps, or mulching in fields

the late summer coastline heaving with heat

*decks almost to the water so heavy with fish, one million landed that day, in that one port.*

# Element 109

All your properties were theft.
You got bent into existence
but you flipped right out again.
There's not even a skid of you
on a laboratory wall. But I like to think
about that place you flipped back in to
where boulders of you populate the plains,
and your hunched nuggets resonate
in cliffs alongside flint and sandstone,
and in your purest form, you have been teased
into fabulously radiating filaments
or used to reinforce the protective tiles
of craft designed to find the planet
you started out on — here — where
it's all too clear you won't collude
in what someone called the tyranny of things.

# Vital capacity

They opened the lung
in search of a tumour
and found a *tree*—

dislodged it,
its alveoli roots,
its ignorant benevolent seed.

A blood-sapling
in a bed of soft blood
that made the headlines.

I thought of this
as I wandered home
down the avenue of throttled limes.

# Pear tree

Worn down by the noise
you take your rifle
and get lucky: pilot
and co-pilot with one bullet.

The chopper tips
into the pear tree out back—
*sching* as a rotor blade
cuts deep into soil

and slices buried brick—
and the pear tree so lovely
at this time of year,
a haunted face of blossom.

# Bigfoot

He squats and rubs his mossy crotch
on the timber stump, leaving the scent-note
that won't be read for a score of Falls.

His tracks are twisted and mighty
between the drifts of open wood that blow
back beyond the range and then beyond that.

Often-times they lead back to the town,
where trashcanned newspaper photos blur
with gasoline and cooking fat.

Holding the ice-cream the kid just dropped,
his tongue, fat and red, violates the melt.
He stows his blood, wields his fob of ferns.

# The city

A gull questions the roof-terrace water-butt
then launches into prayer above the mosque.
Boys on the breakwater aim stones at the grebe.
A cucumber is peeled, cut, salted and handed over.

At Suna's palace by the pier, we eat the best kofte,
eyes salty from last night's raki.
The fishermen pull lines out, sewing up a rent;
sunbathers are crashed into a stern, each wave a new face of the sun.

I was a hooded crow, tumbling and broken as masonry;
I was a seagull, lifting the dome of the mosque with my cries;
I was a twig-legged sparrow, clawing the cobble for a grain of wheat;
I was a jellyfish, washed in from the sea with a crowd of ideas.

I am the knee-joint of the Bosphorus, flexing to another's will.
In the day's heart, evening waits with its sky-leaf folded.

# Shark-watching

Weather report, 15:00:
wind 250°
moderate breeze
(*dust and loose paper raised,*
*small branches begin to move*)
sea state: *wavelets*
*with glassy crests, not breaking*
cloud cover: 100%.
Visibility: Wolf Rock lighthouse
a faint rain-checked mark
15 kilometres offshore.

The watchpoint:
a van parked up a slew of mud
a fold-out chair
a telescope rain-proofed in a black plastic bag
photos for ID
a hemisphere of sea.

Up the coast: the Cape,
Porth Ledden, Zawn Buzz,
down: Maen Dower
then the wash of Whitesand Bay,
the Brisons [say *Briznz*]
set opposite, Little and Great
mistakes of rock,
cormorant roosts.

≈

Where to look for sharks:
the gannet's stab-wound
in the tension of sea

the tide-race slicks
spinning off the shore
where water meets water

(the gannet's slow tweezers
picking out the sprats, the sandeels).

∼

*Have you seen the choughs?*
He knows where they're nesting,
snuck in a credible zawn
three miles up the coast.
They were seen here this morning
the pair of them touching down
and lifting up, cinders,
black with trims of red.

∼

The baskers follow the plankton blooms
fanning out from their winter range
as the summer waters warm
rising from the benthic gloom
to shallows penetrated by the sun
zoning in with *Ampullae of Lorenzini* —
electro-sense — channelling volumes
through their gill-curtained gapes.

∼

That night: the Briznz'
giant double-fin of rock
plunging into the deep
off Karrek Los.

Basking shark counts (max. number visible at surface from watchpoint). Please state whether the same Basking Shark has been seen/recorded more than once.

| Time (24hr) | No. of sharks | Direction and distance from watchpoint (approx.) | Distinctive marks—direction of movement, interesting behaviour |
|---|---|---|---|
| 0530 | 0 | | |
| 0600 | 0 | | |
| 0630 | 0 | | |
| 0700 | 0 | | |
| 0730 | 0 | | |
| 0800 | 0 | | |
| 0830 | 0 | | |
| 0900 | 0 | | |
| 0930 | 0 | | |
| 1000 | 0 | | |
| 1030 | 0 | | |
| 1100 | 0 | | |
| 1130 | 0 | | |
| 1200 | 0 | | |
| 1230 | 0 | | |
| 1300 | 0 | | |
| 1330 | 0 | | |
| 1400 | 0 | | |
| 1430 | 0 | | |
| 1500 | 0 | | |
| 1530 | 0 | | |
| 1600 | 0 | | |
| 1630 | 0 | | |
| 1700 | 0 | | |
| 1730 | 0 | | |
| 1800 | 0 | | |
| 1830 | 0 | | |
| 1900 | 0 | | |
| 1930 | 0 | | |
| 2000 | 0 | | |
| 2030 | 0 | | |

## DAY TWO

Karrek Los (grey rock)
then centuries later
Carn Gluze,
now Carn Gloose.

Weather report:
wind: 240°.
Strong breeze —
*umbrella use difficult*
cloud cover: 100%
visibility: 30m.
Other notes:
sea obscured by fog

*ninety-mile-an-hour fog*

*St Just heat-haze.*

∼

A figure in fog way off
whistles.

The Marseilleise
comes and goes in the wind.

Wind catches on the edge of rock and snags
wind catches on the gorse needles and tears
wind works the heather
plies the lichen
threads the stink of bladderwrack
through vortices of bracken
whispers *bladderwrack and bracken*

*bladderwrack and bracken*
*bladderwrack and bracken.*

Fog motorways up the cliff
from the invisible sea
a gull's vague form
a curl of sea foam.

Behind the fog
a thousand basking sharks
rounding their grey muzzles
on plankton.

∼

That night:
(a clear sky)
grilled mackerel and the Perseids.

## DAY THREE

Weather report:
wind: 200°
sea viscous and bloody
overcast
edge of weather front visible
stationary to northwest.

Isles of Scilly in view.

The legend of Lyonesse:
*nuthn but scrap metal*
*tween here unthe Scillies.*
A wreck the other side u the Briznz

carried fine china
cups and saucers—
£80 if you can pull an unchipped pair
out of the barnacled reef—

*worth a dive.*

The *Minnehaha* ran aground in fog
18 April 1910
on Seal Rock, Isles of Scilly
carrying a cargo
of cattle
(some made it to shore),
Austin 7s,
coconuts
and grand pianos with ivory keys

(*worth a dive*).

~

A bumblebee tumbles
off the Atlantic
and fixes on a gleam of quartz.

~

The wreck of the copper mine
Wheal Alfred
its fathoms and hidden miles
the 5,500 year-old
wreck of the barrow
Ballowall
the wreck of bracken
all along the coast

the Briznz opposite,
catastrophe of rock

(*worth a dive*).

~

One dugong,
one fin whale's gothic arch . . .

~

. . . no shark-fin soup
on the menu today . . .

but wait —
a wavelet far out
stays
solidifies
goes,
breaks again

20 feet between dorsal fin and tail fin
another ten to the nose —
gulping sea, the basker
tracks the plankton cloud
below, close to the watchpoint

huge in the binocular field . . .

not on the menu today.

~

The sharks follow the warm water
where the plankton bloom
moving up the water column.
They cut the sparkling sky
three times: nose, fin, tail.
Fatheaded
the length and weight of a London bus
they tadpole in a huge
brightly-lit green glass vase
somewhere
many miles from here.

∿

Sun-break?
The prospect draws out the tourists.

∿

That night: a dozen wasps in the kitchen.

## DAY FOUR

*Two teenage brothers out on a boat trip got a surprising*
*visit from this massive basking shark (pictured left).*
*Quick-thinking Jake Norris, 15, grabbed his camera*
*and snapped this shot as the gentle beast circled his boat*
*last weekend.*

. . . not on the menu today.

∿

Weather report:
cuttlefish sky
kelp wind

hottentot fig spotted
proliferating
near the shoreline.

Bookmark, 1 p.m.:
a pod of bottlenose dolphins
eight adults and one calf
heading out to Whitesand Bay
pass directly below the cliff.
Two hours later they return
swaggering and bouncing,
swerve round Cape Cornwall
and off towards Pendeen
as the whole coast watches.

≈

Bookmark:
a peregrine
folds itself between
two leaves of wind
and slips into
the distance.

≈

Bookmark:
a kestrel
balances a filled cup
on its back

as it hovers.
Nothing is spilled
even when the beetle stirs.

≈

Baskers by-pass this coast.
They go deep,
mine the seams of sea
nosing the veins that reach
between waters,
that channel nutrients
that feed the plankton.

≈

The geologist is looking for sand
at Porth Nanven.
A norwesterly
took it offshore last winter
*We need an onshore storm to bring it back.*

The Legend of Lyonesse:
from here to the Scillies
*walkable in the Mesolithic.*

≈

By the mine-shaft opening
near six-thousand year-old
Ballowall Barrow,
a toaster, a microwave,
wok, frying pan,
a portrait of Emily
a knotted plastic sack

and below the wire mesh cap
a 200-yard drop
to the worked-out lodes
of Wheal Alfred—
walkable in the Eighteen-Forties.

≈

That night: ivory keys
play
down corridors of sea.

DAY FIVE

7 a.m.: basking shark spotted
500m from watchpoint
close to Cape Cornwall
surface feeding
moving to 280°
observed for five minutes—
so it says in the log-book.

≈

Off Karrek Los
a grey seal, bottling.
Off Gribba Point
a grey seal, bottling.
Off Maen Dower
down in Porth Nanven
down in Priest's Cove
over by the Briznz:
grey seals, bottling.

A black buoy tugging
at its ocean tether
a grey buoy bottling
in a credible zawn
black marker flags
in among the
dark and fin-like waves.

~

A pod of humans in the zawn
including one calf
masked and flippered
making sand-clouds;

a million tiny suns,
the sky reeling;

the Briznz, black
and sharp as mussels.

~

A grey seal bottles for a while
in the zawn below
then moves underwater,
a slow bullet
seen from the watchpoint above.

~

4 p.m.: possible sighting
of basking shark
surface feeding

moving to 280°
slipping through the fin-like waves
becoming waves

a school of thousands.

# The toad of the carn

He sits on the slip of moor, presiding
His skin is granite, with quartzite grain
His mouth is a widening frost-crack
His eye a delta of lichen pouring black

His seethe-bed is heather and moss
His slump is a pile of old stone
His clamminess floods the valley with mist
His tangle-breath stunts oak in the hedgerow

His claw is a rag of wild
His croak is the wind
His pink tongue is the heat of the world

He didn't move when the concrete settling tanks were built beside him
He didn't move when the leylandii along the access road were planted
    and grew above him
He didn't move when the quarry-edge teetered below him
and the sand-burrow tottered over him, convector-steep

His thought is the spill of ravens through air

# Sky burial

On the long grass fields that sweep to the view miles below
of the bay, looking down on the polygon bay and the silent lines

of geometric swell. On the clayrock fields, the rabbit fields,
blaze of gorse-edged burrows and gravelly stent, between

excavations the diamond fields, cider fields, domed in the sky.
With the clouds streaming over on long threads of air, excavations

themselves, and the pit-chaos, the eddy of works in Trenance
and Gunheath, prayers scratched out and panicked in the wind,

bothered by the dark setting sun. Then a kestrel hunting off
the gorsey tips, dark crescent in the sky, sickle ranging the gorse

and grass. And then again a buzzard, the bud on a telegraph pole,
flowering as we approach along the hedgeline.

# Hensbarrow

buzzard in the sky—driftwood—feathers salt-worn—trailing in the
airstream—its body pebbled by the flow—

ocean fragments both sides of the moor—sea bluer than before,
solid blue—keeping watch, waiting—

moorland in-between—sweep of heather and gorse—wide white
tracks—squabbling clutch of cottages—white crossroads—high,
dark, dusty lines of hedge—

scribbling motor noise in the pitworks below—lunar effacement—
the invisible gape of Littlejohns, Gunheath—

Carrancarrow's mountain of dirty salt—the tideline of black gorse
and clitter—the grim reflection of sky—

the buzzard taloned—showing its scarlet mew—distant *killas* gaudy
in the sun—tiny bright hedges and farms

# Blackbird (slight return)

You are the combination lock
You are the scurry of the sky

You are a flicker in dark glass
You are the dusk's only echo

# New Year's Eve, St Ives

The night as well was cloaked with rain
not its true self at all
when we left the phantom room behind
to roam the clots of ghouls

and striding down the miles to shore
the headlights poured light on
the cliff, the beach and a panda bear
making two backs with a nun.

# Painting the Clay

white with a hint of gorse-tinder
white with a hint of machine oil
white with a rhododendron gloss
white with a hint of clay-rock canyon
white with a hint of peacock butterfly
on a glint of quartz

powder white and copper quarry-lake
poisoned mud white
creamy white with a hint of mica
quartz white with a hint of sky

white with a hint of clitter on the sea-ward moor
white with a hint of clatter of falling rocks
tiny white with a shadow of slow wing turning
bone white with a blush of clay marrow

gorse haze at dusk white
mud-white
boot-white
fading night white

white with a hint of Nanpean clay-dries
white with a hint of Foxhole mica-dam

white with a hint of what happened
up Chegwins Farm

# The Map of Clay

Tips, transmission mast
china clay works (dis)
dismantd rly, disused workings
adit (dis), disused workings

China Clay Works (disused)
tip, tip, pit (dis)
FB, resr, quarry (dis)
Experimental Seeding Grounds

Adits, Chy, Mica Dam
vertical face, sand and shingle
quarry (dis) edged with cliff
Great Longstone China Clay Works

Trelavour Downs (dismantd)
Halvignan farm (dismantd)
the village of Retew (dismantd)
the hamlet called *America* (dismantd)

Blooms of unmapped white,
eddies of industrial workings
Longstone Downs (dismantd)
the longstone *dismantd*

Tips (dis) Carluddon Farm
Tips (dis) Carbis Common
Watch Hill lopped and crowned with stent
Hensbarrow checked and topped with stent

Smash-patterns of early fields
logging huge primeval clitter
the spreading white of china clay works
soothing the old fidgety land

Carranca-X
Caerlo-X
X-loggas
X-namarth

# Fal

The sea pushes inland from Carrick Roads,
pushes up between the oaky banks
of Polgerran, Borlase, then Lamorran,

the tide's slide swoons over silt
and shingle, up the continent's recoil,
its tidy increment of slab and soil,

a lid closing on the river's eye;
the ocean makes the contours'
dream a dream of filling mud,

darkness in a bowl of sky. At tidal reach,
the loud sibilants of Sett Bridge
wake it, and the water stops and slacks—

though a rumour of salt works on up
following the stream through cowfields
curling through the trackless mesh of woods

up past Creed and Golden, further on
past Kernick mica dam and Virginia
to the river's nervous source—

even the long-horned cattle there, below
the clay hills' powder-blast, feel its sleepiness
somewhere in their swim of grass.

# Pertaining to the cod

The story went that in those days a man could reach from his flat-hulled dory, search the heavy water, eyes closed, and pull one out. He could step into a shoal and balance on the fish's backs, dance on their upturned snouts as more came to the light, surrounding with their opened mouths. A deft-footed boy could run the cod-backs with a message, following their stepping stones to shore, sunshine spinning off the mud-coloured slabs before they could turn and sink. The waves as they broke were a surge of cod, tanked from trough to crest with glints and glassy eyes. The story went that in those days the sea was thick and game as pie, dense with cod-meat, stuffed with plankton jelly. But now we zoom across the thinnest consomme, this clear cold unassembled water, making brief froth in our scouring wake, our 50-knot launch and its silence and noise, its coast-and-flap, coast-and-flap, and deep below us, snow crab blindly prise atmospheres apart, sorting through the debris of those days.

# Scope of Clay

| | |
|---|---|
| farmed-out farms | named of stone |
| guilt of mists | cultivate dock |
| dusk-stand of foxgloves | pivot of moor |
| *Biscovillack* | *Goonamarth* |
| | |
| clay-powdered oaks | buzzard watch |
| cauldron of shouts | freaked with gorse |
| the pit advancing | punch of water |
| *Burngullow* | *Cocksbarrow* |
| | |
| open pit-gape | spiral stope |
| closed-down rock | piled-up stent |
| in the distance | a dress of waves |
| *Goodbye Carran-* | *Carrancarrow* |

# The New World

Raining for several days, the tubes all flooded,
the streets steaming, the air close to liquid,

we slipped into the New World
and ordered dim sum.

The waitress arrived from the middle distance
squeaking past the fish tank towards us

her trolley laid with sudden demons,
heavy wishes from the dim fathoms.

An undisciplined muster: *har gow* weighted
like shoreline purses, soft-coiled in muslin;

won tons still reeling from the deep-fry,
their crispy skirts sequinned with oil;

nameless dumplings of glutinous dough,
each drum its own sumptuous midden.

We launched them into our throats,
eased their crackling,

tested their taut presumptions,
sat through their seminar of odds.

And when the lid of rain had lifted, we left, dabbing
the sweet and sour of the street-lit night.

# Automotive

Fall, and the car is a leaf in a drift of leaves
mulching in the suburban turning.
Wing-mirrors are web-slung, hide-holes doze with spiders,
dew studs the alloy shell, rigid drops of $H_2O$
hugging the sprayed out, stress-tested ribs and veins.
All the autumn cars are safe as sleeping river-trout
sunk in the dappled lull of a woodland stream,
dreaming of torque, grip, blurred hedges, roads.

In winter the car magics frost from the air
and it grows in barbs and cross-hatch, mending the worries in the shine
that to a human eye are imperceptible—
though where the metalwork's thatch of atoms absolutely holds
the frost spins, pirouettes and pearls, extemporising like a happy child.
Then ignited, the car rouses with a burst of song
and becomes a shape of hot air restoring its plush of glass.
It's an advent of capacity and acceleration,
doors open with proposals and miles-per-gallon.

*Slick summer tyres stowed*
*all packed up for the trip, fluids topped off, got snowchains,*
*snow shovel, tow ropes, bandsaw,*
*sledgehammer, axe, dirty great mud terrain tyres . . .*

When the automotive world turns again, the car is sharp as a laugh in spring,
a sheer of light, a safe bullet, the carved droplet falling along
the highway's fast curve, pushing storms aside.
Then in summertime, the sun's unalloyed iris parks in the toughened glass.
Lime-sap bastes the metalwork, flies snag on the matt hull.
The upholstery sweats and smarts as it waits.

So let's go for a drive: unpark, gather speed along the open road,
aim to strait a mountain, breach the glacier-head,
give the car its mood of alp and marmot-shock.
Handbreak-turn the National Gallery, gatecrash the Jubilee line

and force the rush hour back,
by-pass the rules and run the wrong-way streets ragged and mad.
Then leave the car to glory, unpeopled, in its own sense of light.
The streetlamps bend to see it roll from the tarmac dark—
a fossil with subtle, treasured vertebrae—
carve itself from the cliff face, stone in a drift of stone.

# Abandon

On the scanty margin of a minor road, a workman's glove,
still pumped, one finger beckoning, tracks you

as you pass. A few miles on, its twin, tread-marked
with dust, crawls on all fives from a tide of litter.

A single scuffy trainer is half-ploughed into an open field;
a sandal in another surfaces from loam.

Two shoes, laces tied, are their own slung broadcast on the telegraph line;
a mint bobble-hat unknits on the needle of a park's December.

And the night-beach covets a pair of shorts, a set of bra and pants,
the ocean's sparkling threads, the stitchwork of stars.

# Arrest

Between the ocean's push up the black pebble shore
and its heavy drag back down:

a snorkeler's flukes stopped still in their dive
as two fingers with nothing to hold

a red-legged crab edging the rock
with one painted nail still in view

a young man primed on a high seaward ledge
to tombstone into the waves

two claws of cloud clutched venomously
at the mountain's gravel throat

and the wind, speed-reading your abandoned romance,
bookmarking this break in the plot.

# Ascent

As sure as the first cock-crow of dawn
will come before the last dog-bark of dusk
and for every one mosquito smudged
to a micro-pall of brown-black blood
a dozen more will rise from the mire's dark,
in my half-sleep tonight I'll dream again
of this island's birth from liquid fire—
sprung stone squeezed through boiling brine
wrinkling, twisting like an eyeless pup,
the volcano building its shadow over the sea
then settling, cooling, greening . . . and then the fruit:
hotels along the lava-black beaches.

When I wake, the air is fraught with fennel-scent
tumbling down the valley into the waves.

# OS (slight return)

flesh and grey the innocent estates

thick blue, M, thick red, dual carriageway, thin orange, generally
more than 4m wide

a cross as a site of antiquity, the sails of a windmill, sails of a
windpump, sails of a wind generator, place of worship

the pathway toggles over fields, moving over contours, clicking
on and off

undetectable as a destination, rabbits sing in expressions of grass

trees mouth the ground's longing for sky

fate works its parts-per-billion, surging up the food chain,
accumulating blood lines, jigging veins off course

information not available in uncoloured areas

# Acknowledgements

Acknowledgements and thanks are due to the editors of *Magma*, *The North*, *nth position*, *Poetry Wales*, *Rialto* and *Smiths Knoll* where some of these poems were first published. 'Automotive' began life as a collaboration with Camellia Stafford. Thanks to Kristian Petterson, Gideon Simeloff and Patrick Brandon for their invaluable advice on the manuscript, to Roddy Lumsden for his expert guidance, and most of all to Anne Kazimirski for her encouragement and love.

James Goodman's evocative first collection is warm and inventive, dramatic and ethically-charged, picking its way through the clay country of mid-Cornwall as it tackles the ecological pressures on the natural world. Many of the poems take their inspiration from the scale and force of landscape, finding a unifying beauty in its geology, the maps that describe it and the industries that exploit it for mineral wealth. But this collection also ranges widely in subject, and includes poems on birds, sharks, deer, fish, limoncello, dimsum and the North American Bigfoot. Goodman balances the gravity of some of his observations with comedy and lightness of touch, which all lovers of poetry will find endearing and enlightening

"These are poems crafted to match the physical nature and power of Cornwall's post-industrial landscape, rich with awareness of the fractured histories that define this region far off the tourist trail. Cornwall's mineral, maritime and moorland realities are present here in a vital and present-day idiom, shot through with tough and compelling lyricism. An exciting and thoughtful debut."
— PENELOPE SHUTTLE

"Where you or I might look at a thing, or be in a place, and think no more of it, James Goodman cannot help but write poetry about it. And the poetry is vital and succulent and makes you revel in the lusciousness of words, the deliciously unexpected metaphor, his magical handling of mystery where we thought there was none. Nor is he too earnest for a snigger and a giggle, for there is laughter in there too, and deftly crafted ecstasy and euphoria. For poems replete with zawn and clitter, there's nobody quite like him. Buy it; read it; and if you're like me, you'll love it." — CHRIS STEWART

*James Goodman grew up in St Austell, Cornwall, near the Clay Country landscapes described in* Claytown. *He works for a sustainable development charity and lives in Hertfordshire with his wife and son. This is his first collection.*

ISBN 978-1-84471-259-5

http://www.saltpublishing.com

SALT